HOW TO GET A GUY TO LOVE YOU

Your Guide To Getting Your Prince Charming

By

Claire Robin

Copyright

All rights reserved. No part of this publication **How to Get a Guy to Love You** may be reproduced, stored in a retrieval system or transmitted in any form or by any means - electronic, mechanical, photocopying, recording, and scanning without permission in writing by the author.

ZeroNever Publishing House

USA | UK | Canada

Table of Contents

Copyright 2

CHAPTER 1 - Introduction 4

CHAPTER 2 - Getting Ready For The Battle 5

Becoming the better person 6

Be an unforgettable woman! 13

Make room for him 16

Throw out everything that can prevent him from falling in love with you..17

CHAPTER 3 - Evaluate Your Target 19

Create your man 19

Is he truly your dream man and his he worth this sacrifice? 21

How to know how much he values your presence 24

CHAPTER 4 - Attracting Him 27

How to get him to notice you 27

Questions that may help check your progress.............35

CHAPTER 5 - Taking What Belongs To You......................37

Use your strength to make him yours.........................37

CHAPTER 6 - How To Become His Unforgettable Woman 41

What to do while waiting for prince charming to make up his mind...46

CHAPTER 7 – Final Move 50

CHAPTER 1 - Introduction

Love can be so amazing; the tingling feeling it gives just can't let you stay calm. It is always a nice experience to fall head over heels for someone and when they reciprocate the love, it feels like life has just become perfect.

However, life has not always been that simple. There are times we fall in love and realize we are falling alone; the other party does not even consider being anything more than just a friend. Also, there are times when the people we want so badly need us even more.

As uncertain as it can be, the idea of love gets better when we know we do not have to lose everyone that does not reciprocate our feelings in the first instance because there is a way to get them to think more than twice about us. It is true we cannot get everyone to love us, but what is the harm if we try?

This guide will help you get that undying love from that man you so desire and if he does not yield, he will definitely hate himself when he realizes he has lost his chance. You are strong, you have that power. Now, let's go get him.

CHAPTER 2 - Getting Ready For The Battle

ove is war and choosing to love is a big decision. So before getting into a thing as big as love, it is important for you to fortify yourself. There are a lot of important things to be done before bringing in Prince Charming and we will be discussing some of the important ones. You will be surprised that having it right in this aspect alone is enough to get you any man of your choice. So, to prepare yourself for Prince Charming, you have to

Becoming the better person

There are many reasons you lost your ex; some may have been his fault and the others, yours. Now, since you are aiming for a fresh start and a major catch, you must be sure you do not make the same mistakes again. Becoming a better person needs just as much effort as beautifying a house does. At the end of the day, you will always look at the mirror and appreciate the person you have so become.

So, how do you get better and improve yourself for Prince Charming? The answer is simple; follow this guide.

Tips for self-improvement

- **Be your most valuable asset**

You may be one of those screaming self-crush on social media or you may have friends who do. Good, but it does not just end at the screams. Loving yourself is the greatest thing you can do as long as you are alive. If you fail here, then you have failed in life.

Have you ever wondered about the dangers of not loving yourself? Well if you have not, let me help you. When you do not love yourself, the whole world will stampede on you; and you will wake up one day to realize that you are now the person that tries to please every other person apart from yourself.

The reason you swallowed your ex-lover's mess is that you loved him more than you loved yourself. This is the danger!

Until you put yourself first and do every good thing needed to be comfortable, you will always be nothing but a doormat for people; not just men.

I am not saying you should not be kind; you should be and in addition to that, you should love everyone in the world but that should come after you have loved yourself. Chances are the world will not even appreciate your love.

You do not have to have a voice like Celine Dion to be perfect neither do you need to have a butt like Nikki Minaj to be adored. All you need to be enough is yourself because you are perfect the way you are.

- **Never blink where your health is concerned**

Health is wealth and as a better person, you need to have good health. Without good health, you will not even be able to enjoy the presence of prince charming in your life. So now, how do you attain this state of great health?

Step up your nutrition

It is easy to stuff in the junk foods than going through the whole hectic process to get some more nutritious diet. However, your bodies will always pay for it. The effects of sugar and processed foods can never be overemphasized and as a woman who loves herself, reducing the amount you take can be one of the best ways to show your self-love.

I know you may be a career woman and you barely have time to put your meals together; sigh! I know just how you feel but if you want to stay healthy chasing that dream and getting yourself that happy man, you will need to stay safe from these dangers.

Replace snacks with fruits and drink a lot of water. You will love your new look and vitality than the sweetness of chocolate.

Get a healthy dose of exercise

Do you have that dream shape and the weight you want to attain? Now is the best time to get it. If you are already having the shape and healthy weight you have always admired, maintain it. Exercise is the best way to help you have a healthy mind and body, especially when combined with a healthy diet.

Is there a man you are trying to forget? Take him (in your mind) to the treadmill and run like you are running all over him. When you are done, you will feel better (like you just kicked his ass) and your body will be refreshed. Research has also shown that some exercises can help us get rid of unhealthy emotions. Get them and try them out so they can help purge out all the garbage from your mind.

- **Replace terrible habits with new ones**

We are our habits and our habits are a reflection of who we are. Are you getting better? Let your habits show it. It is easy to develop funny habits and routines since they are easier to stick to but forming new habits can seem difficult. However, habits do not just go, they get replaced!

It is believed that doing something for 21 days automatically turns them into habits. Write down the habits that make your life far from being beautiful and write down new better activities to replace them. Try doing these new things for 21 days and watch them becoming solid milestones in your life.

Habits and routines can make waking up one of the most boring occurrences. To get this desired change, write down a number of things you like to be doing in the morning; be realistic about them. This will not only make you eager to wake up, but it will also help you start up your day on the right foot.

- **Let go of the past**

The past can be beautiful in reminiscence but not as a place to live the present and maybe the future. Keeping memories of how beautiful or terrible the past was can hinder you from getting the needed joy and achievement from today. Your past can even affect your ability to get and keep Prince Charming. As we progress, you will find out how the past can hinder his love for you.

- **Read**

Reading does not only help you pass an exam, but it also makes you sound like the person you have always admired. Reading stimulates the mind and builds vocabulary; it gives you more interesting ideas on things to talk about. There are a lot of self-improving books you can consume; novels will also do you much good.

When you read, you will give Prince Charming what to be wowed about. Never forget the power of the first impression. Read so that you will give him what to dream of when you are gone.

If you are the busy type and you are wondering how to create some time to read, try this: Simply take out 30 minutes of your time before going to bed to read. If watching the television will take that time, turn it off and do everything you can to read every night before going to bed.

If you have a poor reading habit, doing this will also be helpful. Do not forget it takes about 21 days to develop a good trait.

- **Refresh your mind**

As long as you are alive, you will always come in contact with negative emotions. Someone will die, another will annoy you, a friend will leave and most of the time, you will be caught up in the holdup when you are trying to meet up with a very important meeting. Things will always happen to ruin your day but the way you respond to them is what determines the quality of life you live.

Seeing life through the negative lens and letting everything find its way into our heart will eventually turn you into an angry negative person but learning to let things go and having a better view of everything will make life happier and worthwhile.

Life will always pose challenges but these challenges will turn into stepping stones if you see and handle them with the eye of positivity.

- **Manage your friend list**

Your level of positivity and self-improvement has a lot to do with the friends you keep. If you keep positive and successful people as friends, you will find yourself drifting towards success and positivity but if it is the other way round, I am sure you know what the result will be.

Now, take a book and write down the names of your friends and critically examine their quality of life. Is it the kind you will like to have? If you were a man, would you like to accept that? Your answer should determine if you should keep them or let them go.

- **Have a "me-time"**

This is the time for self-assessment. After trying out all of these steps; make out time for yourself and evaluate your quality of life. How much improvement have you made so far? How are your grades? Did you get a recommendation at work? What about your health? Have you been able to keep up with a healthy diet and exercise?

The answers to this question will help you know if you are growing into the person you wanted or if you are really derailing.

Love can be found when sought from the right platform. Before inviting Prince Charming in, make sure you are right enough to be his Mrs. Right. To progress on preparing yourself to gain the love of your Prince Charming, consider the next step.

Be an unforgettable woman!

This guy in question has met thousands of women in his life and as long as he lives, he will keep meeting them. Many liked him, many are and a lot are willing to go a mile extra than you are just to keep him. Now the question is how do you get him to overlook this kind of competition and will his life to you? It's simple; be the woman he can never forget. Work your way into his mind and keep yourself there forever. If he can't get you out of his head, he'll never be able to keep you out of his life.

So now, here's the serious question:

Who is an unforgettable woman?

An unforgettable woman is a 'whole woman'. She is the woman that has her life and sets out to live it. Have you ever seen a girl that you think is out rightly weird but she doesn't give a shit about what you have to say? That's a whole woman. Being whole means being complete in yourself; it means having your own definition of life and living it like it is no man's business.

To be whole means you have so improved yourself in such a way that the only option left for people is to love you for being you. A whole woman has a career or is working towards it. She has her own set of rules and does not blink at anyone who tries to break or adjust its borders. Does she have a hobby? Of course, she does and she goes all out to have fun.

A whole woman is also a kind woman who can give the overflowing love from her cup to her partner in such a way that it fills him till he's got no space to go hunting for more. That's a woman who is whole and whole women are never forgotten.

There is an irresistible attraction for whole women. This is because she is confident in herself and to a man, confidence is sexier than lingerie. The following are the reasons men never let whole women go:

- Men love freedom and they believe that with a whole woman, they can still have time for themselves since she will sometimes be busy doing the things she loves.
- They believe she knows who she is and so she'll understand when he's joking and will know how to play along
- He knows she won't swallow his shit. This will always keep him on his toes to be a better person.
- She has a life and can help him build his.
- She knows her value and will not give him a chance to make her feel otherwise, etc.

These kinds of women are few in the world today and this has made men climb mountains and cross uncountable seas just to find a woman with this kind of 'class". So, if women of this class are few, what do you think your prince charming will do when he finds you? Of course, he will become your puppet and will do everything within his power and a little outside it to make you his forever. However, there is a little more to be done.

Make room for him

End those conversations now, end them. Let your exes know it is finally over and you can no longer continue with the breakup sex. The casual sex partners too should be thrown outside the gate. You cannot let them choke prince charming with all you are going through to get him.

If there is any that won't let you have peace, block him and refuse to feel guilty about it. The future is too bright for people like him to destroy.

If you had any strings of anger tying you with one of the souls of your past lover, cut it now! If you were wrong, you can arrange for lunch and apologize. However, if you know that meeting him again can lead you back to his bed, do it on the phone. Keeping the distance will prevent the plasters from falling on your neighbors downstairs.

When they are all gone from your mind, prevent new ones from coming in. Stay focus and keep your mind on getting the bird.

This newly created space will make him feel safe being with you.

Throw out everything that can prevent him from falling in love with you

This is very important. In getting a man to fall head over heels for you, you must be able to get him to place you on a pedestal. This means that he should not find anything disgusting about you. I know everyone has a flaw but your own flaws must not be so loud to get him running.

Keep a clean home and never forget to do your laundry. Take out the old shabby underwear and never let him set his eyes on them by mistake. Clear out your cupboard but above all, never forget to clear out your past.

When clearing your physical cupboard, it is important for you to consider clearing the emotional cupboard too. Throw out every wrong notion you had about men. It will not do you any good with Prince Charming. It will keep you from accepting him and that will eventually drive him away.

The past hurts will not do you any good either. You have to let them go so you do not mistakenly punish Peter for the sins of Paul.

What power does the past have over getting the love of your prince charming?

A lot! If your prince charming finds out about the number of exes you have had exceeds an expected figure, it could turn him off. Imagine him finding out that you have seriously dated 8 guys already. What does that mean to him? To him, that means that

- Eight guys have humped you and if each of them were able to get into you about 20 times, that's 20 X 8 = 160 times other men have been inside you. Sweetheart, it is not as funny as it sounds.
- For eight consecutive times, you failed to make a relationship work. This will make him wonder what the 8 guys saw that made them leave. Believe me, you could not have lost all of them because they were all jerks.
- He may just end up losing out as the other eight did.

Imagine these reasons; they are enough to make a guy change his mind about you forever. So to avoid a scenario like this, take out the pictures of your exes; yes, even the one you loved so much and never let him see it; at least he should not see them displayed on the wall. If he asks you about your past relationships, tell him 'there is nothing interesting about them'. That will get him on his toes to make this one interesting.

CHAPTER 3 - Evaluate Your Target

Create your man

Now you have made yourself an unforgettable woman, you must have the kind of man you want. You just don't deserve anything. You can start by picking the qualities you want to see in him. You want a funny man, feel free to expect from him.

There are a lot of perfect qualities a man can have that can make a relationship really interesting. If you are having difficulties putting together the qualities you need from a man, take a paper and a pen and try to pick any of the following qualities you think your man should have:

Some outstanding masculine qualities

Alert	Artistic	Articulate	Agile	Attentive
Bold	Brave	Bright	Brilliant	Business oriented
Calm	Caring	Charming	Cheerful	Comforting
Decent	Devoted	Discipline	Dependable	Dignified
Elegant	Eloquent	Educated	Enthusiastic	Exuberant

These qualities are just a few of the expected qualities of a cool guy. With this, you can get more to have a better picture of the man you want.

When planning for Prince Charming, it is important you know that he may not possess all the qualities you expect but if he possess up to 60%, you are good to go. If he does not, and your heart does not feel okay about him, walk and wait till you meet another; never settle for less. As an unforgettable woman, the power you have in this game is self-confidence.

Is he truly your dream man and is he worth this sacrifice?

Have you heard of women who sacrifice their lives for some guy who ended up dumping them and walking away? What do you think was the underlying cause of it?

There will always be a great risk of disappointment when you go through hell to get the love of a man who only turns out to be a nightmare. So, dear, I know you are really eager to learn how to nail him down but before that, check if he has your expected qualities; and examine with the following to examine him to be sure he is worth this love you have to offer.

Who is the man deserving of your love?

A man that deserves the love of a quality woman like you is one who can love, protect and provide for you and value your presence. As a man, if he cannot do these three things, then you do not need to undergo this mission for him.

Now, let us look at these attributes one after the other:

i. **Love**

Before trying to get this man to love you, you have to find out if he is capable of love. Ask about his previous relationships and be sure of his records (watch out, he will try to lie). If you realize he is the cheating kind, or he has a record of a playboy, run. Run dear; do not even try to change him because you won't. You will only end up hurting yourself.

Love has a great deal to do with respect. The man that deserves you is one that has respect for women. If he talks rudely to women or sounds insolent about feminism, get a change of mind. That kind of man will not respect you neither will he respect your presence in his life.

ii.   Protection

Now, why does a man protect a lady? Love is never complete if you have no need to preserve what is yours. As a man, it is in his gene to keep the "fragile" woman he loves (in his little mind) safe from the wolves (his friends, other guys who he thinks are better than he is and possibly the desperate girls who would do anything to get him) out there.

So how do you know this man will be a good protector? He will keep every other girl at arm's length especially when there is a woman in his life. You see, that's why it is very important to run a background check on this man.

iii. Provision

Exactly! Who needs a man who can't provide? I don't mean a man with the 'not so high' finances; I mean one who does not care about your needs let alone trying to help you get them.

This may not be easy to know since you may not be so close to him but it is a thing to look out for even when you have begun a relationship with him. If for any reason whatsoever, you realize he skips provision; run.

iv.   Valuing your presence

When a man values your presence, he will do everything to keep you around. He will do the sensible things you demand and will stop at nothing to make you feel comfortable with him. This man will cross the deserts just to have your attention and will not let anything make you feel staying with him is a mistake. Is that not sweet?

However, you may not be able to know how much of your presence a guy values till you two get to know each other. But in the beginning, these few signs will help you.

How to know how much he values your presence

- He enjoys your company and tries to get the most out of it
- He pays attention when you talk to him and does not interrupt when you speak
- He makes up reasons to be with you
- He returns your calls when he misses them and apologizes for them
- He apologizes when he is wrong and tries to avoid the same mistake

If he does these things and you think he is deserving of you, proceed to evaluate his eligibility as your prince charming. This eligibility has so much to do with how ready he is to be a prince charming himself.

Is he ready to be a man for you?

Men are careful people where their emotions are concerned and they love to be ready in every aspect before thinking of partnering with a woman. For a man, there are many things that come first in his life apart from a woman and before he can pay attention to you, he must have the following things in place:

a) His purpose

A man's life is not complete without purpose and when he has not found his path in life, he will never be able to be that responsible man you wanted him to be. Is there a time you dated a guy in high school and all he did was act like a jerk as the relationship progressed? What was the cause of it?

Purpose, he was probably on his way to finding why he is really alive and since he did not know it, he was unable to decide if he needed you in his life or not.

So, to stop that from being a second experience, I ask you to evaluate him to know if he really has what drives him. If he does not, abort this mission now!

b) His finances

I have met a lot of girls who failed to look at the financial stability of a man before committing themselves to him. I know you can imagine how some of them ended. A man will only let in a woman he loves when he is sure he can provide for her. This does not mean that financially unstable guys do not truly love; they do but they will not want to commit since they know they are not up to the task financially.

Some guys can even capitalize on their financial instability to drain a woman. They will so get you to believe you are investing in them and at the end of the day, they will walk away. I know there are a few exceptions but being the one financing the relationship will cause it to be unbalanced. Here is the reason:

Men are naturally designed to be providers and as long as you are the one providing, they will keep feeling less manly and without his masculinity, he can't thrive in a relationship. As we progress, you will understand how you can use this aspect of masculinity to get his love and keep it for life.

How does this affect your decision to either go after him or not?

If you know you didn't come all the way down here to just attract a guy and then toss him aside after a few months and since you are definitely putting so many efforts into getting him, he must be worth the stress.

If your prince charming falls short in any of these factors, retract your steps and reconsider what you are really getting into. If it happens that you find out he no longer turns you on or has some qualities that make you doubt his capability of being the man you have always wanted, abort the mission.

Your gut is your greatest gift in this battle, and if your gut warns you against it, please do not continue. It does not matter if he fulfills every requirement for being fought for. Your guts can never be wrong.

CHAPTER 4 - Attracting Him

Now you are ready to put yourself out there and grab a share of what is truly yours. Do not forget what you have learned so far and always remember to put on your confidence daily as a sexy perfume.

How to get him to notice you

Where do you easily find him? Is it his workplace or a social gathering? Wherever it may be, find yourself an excuse to appear there. Before getting there,

a) Look your best:

Looking your best has to do with you taking good care of yourself and wearing the best version of the things you have. Come to think of it; will you even be attracted to him if he looks like a dunghill? Of course not so that will be the same for him. If you look less than you should (based on your income), he will simply look the other way.

I know I shouldn't be overemphasizing this since as an unforgettable woman you have learned what it means to love yourself. Your looks express who you are on the inside. If you look shabby, it will mean that you are not diligent and so nothing is important to you; not even your health.

Your health is important and will always show in the way you look. Terrible nutrition will make your skin and hair look terrible. Mind what you eat and try to keep fit. Let the gym be your friend and if you just can't go there, run around your area till the very ground you tread upon miss you the day you skip. Remember, you are not just doing this for him, you are keeping yourself free from the most dreadful diseases; you know them by name.

To look your best, follow these guidelines:

- Try the feminine hairstyles, they never stop making guys look your way more than once.
- If makeup is your thing, keep it simple but good enough to make you look happy.
- Your teeth and nails should not be left out. Make them important parts of your personal hygiene.
- Do your laundry. Iron the things you have to wear and stitch up the slightest tear.
- Be decent. If you must expose, it should be just a little. Showing 75% of everything can make him think you are desperate and will certainly leave nothing to his imagination.

b) Be approachable

Oh! The heavens forbid you made yourself an epitome of beauty and a masterpiece set on a pedestal and yet, be dreadful and unapproachable. What a wasted effort that would have been.

Tough guys fear! Yes, they do. So, you have to be sure that you are creating some spaces for the Prince Charming to come in. I said Prince Charming, not the bastards on the street! So now, how can our sexy boss get Prince Charming in?

Smile, it will ease his tension. Occasionally glance at him with a soft smile and every once in awhile, fix a gaze. To him, this means 'I won't bite if you say hi'. However, ensure you do not overdo it; that will make him think you are head over heels for him (you and I know you are but that should be our little secret).

He will probably gather some balls to talk to you. When he does, be kind, respectful and smart. Your conversations should tell him you are available, but please, mind your words; they should not sell you off as a gate widely open to receive anything the streets can offer.

But now, it's not just about smiling and getting him to talk to you is not a guarantee that he will. If he must look your way, something must turn his neck and that thing is as simple as the next step.

c) Be different

Come on, I know you are already running your mind on how to be different from every other person especially if they are mostly good. Don't kill yourself over this; the solution is in you, not the girl in your choir or the slay queen in your neighborhood.

Everybody is created differently and there can only be the one you in the world. So, the only way you can successfully be different is by being **you;** the real you. In this business, no faking or pretense is needed; be the best of you and he'll love you for it.

What if you have been battered and bruised? Don't worry, through away the self-pity and pick up your broken pieces; he'll appreciate the strong woman you are.

Bring out your beauty like fine gold; get a life, be happy with yourself, be your best you can be and when he sees you are working your way to the top, he'll be tempted to help you get there. Sorry, I didn't tell you men love being 'the savior of the day'.

There must be something you are good at, do it and let him be amazed at the wonderful talent you are. When you do, feel free to glance at him **shortly** and give a soft smile. Immediately after this 'short glance' please look and walk away. If he must talk to you, let his legs bring him your direction.

d) **Be kind to everyone**

When I was in grade school, we used rudeness to portray strength; we even had this habit of being rude to the boy we are eying. This gave the boys the idea that we had developed some itchiness for them and with that, they bluffed. But this is not a grade school; you have grown and so have the boys and now, they have known what they truly need from a woman.

Though being rude to the guy when he screws up can get him aligned and make him realize you do not swallow his shit, doing it when he is not wrong will give him a terrible perspective of you. Men love respect and they will not tolerate any woman that disrespects them (especially when they are not wrong and sometimes when they are). You have to know what a battle is and what it is not.

Being rude is usually an expression of inner bitterness. When you are rude to people, your prince charming will see this and presume that you are either bitter or have emotional problems. The best any of them can do is to keep you at the least position of attracting him. Sooner or later, he will start planning on how to avoid you so he does not have a share in your bitterness.

e) Give yourself a good carriage

Remember those scattered steps you do and call walking? Throw them away. Price charming must never see that. I know you are living your life for yourself but I am sure you will feel good when you take a glance at the mirror when you walk past and realize you are walking like a queen. The queenly steps will give him a queenly idea of you.

With the wonderful personality you have developed, a queenly walk will do nothing but add to your pride. Your steps will look better with stilettoes but if you only get to see him during a casual outing, leave the stilettoes at home.

Questions that may help check your progress

Question: he barely looks my direction; it's so hard to fix a gaze. What should I do?

Answer: if you have tried all we have discussed here and you do not even catch him for once stealing a glance at you, it could be that he is not just interested. You don't have to force yourself. But if you still want to try you can walk up to him and start a conversation. If he cannot see you by himself, you may want to turn his neck.

Question: he seems interested but I think he is too shy to say anything

Answer: if he is shy to make the first move, keep your cool and if an opportunity shows itself, let your countenance put him at ease. If you feel okay being the first to say hi, please do but just don't try to force a conversation.

Question: I tried to initiate a conversation but he does not seem to pay attention

Answer: this could be caused by two reasons. It could be that you probably caught him at the wrong time when he is busy trying to figure out something else or, he could be that he is not just interested.

If he acts rudely or does not seem to show any interest, drop it and walk away. If he is responsible enough, he will find you and apologize. If he does not, what do you want him for anyway?

Questions: he ignores my messages and calls. What should I do?

Answers: if he ignores your messages and calls, it's because he does not have an interest in you. The only thing you can do about this is to stop trying; I know it will be hard. There are great guys out there who will do anything to get your attention. Let your heart be open; you never can tell who you will meet tomorrow.

Question: I don't think I'm good enough for him, what should I do?

Answer: you should not be asking this question by now. You are more than enough for anyone and if you love yourself enough, that should make you sufficient for any man. The first principle is to be confident enough to love yourself; that's all you need to do.

CHAPTER 5 - Taking What Belongs To You

I f he did not give a good response to the above steps; it may be time to abort the mission but if his response was good and he is beginning to find a friend in you, know that he is interested. And if he is,

Use your strength to make him yours

a) Get 'him' to meet 'you'

This is your chance girl; it may be the only chance you have to show him what you've got on the inside. This period usually comes either when you first meet or during your first serious conversation. Whenever the opportunity presents itself, take it and show him who he should dream of being with.

When you talk, sweetly weave your personality and special abilities into the discussion. For instance, if you were talking about how people react when they get angry, you can jokingly say '…for me, when I get angry, I play the piano'. Wow! You just told him you are a serene and creative lady who doesn't have the time to shout and cry but can convert your hurt into an inspiration. Who wouldn't want to be with such a lady?

b) Play casual

Showing how serious you can be here will not get you the relationship. I know it can help show him how much standard you have but it will not help you grow his love. A man needs to know he can be free to play and joke around in a respectable manner with a girl he wants to love.

If he does not have that confidence to play with you, know that you have lost him. Feel free to be causal and weird (within the confinement of responsibility) and you will give him the confidence to be the same.

Also, as long as he has not used the term "girlfriend" on you, forbid yourself from using it with him; I said, do not try it. If you have your way, be casual enough that you do not give him a clue that marriage could be a good idea to you not to talk of babies. When the time comes, he will be the one begging you to consider them with him.

c) Crawl under him so deep till he loses his ability to forget you

Men are different and so are their needs, this means to have and keep your prince charming, you have to be the unforgettable woman meant for him; not just for the general public. So now, how do you become **his** unforgettable woman?

CHAPTER 6 - How To Become His Unforgettable Woman

There are many great unforgettable women who were never able to attract their prince charming let alone have their love to keep. Others did but lost it with time. I know you don't want to end like them so to have a successful love story, you should learn how to attract and keep a man while still being an unforgettable woman.

Men and women have their own set of rules and definitions of who an unforgettable woman is but to win a man's heart, you have to know how to use your newly found personality to get the love of your life. The following steps will help you:

- **Be playful**

Playful women light up a men's world. Smile brightly and know just how to make the atmosphere light. Be the person he runs to for happiness whenever the world throws him a punch. Let him find joy in you.

You do not have to be totally weird to make him laugh, just be happy yourself and since happiness is contagious, he will find his way to tap from you.

- **Know more about what he does**

Knowing more about your dream man's career will help you know how to keep a conversation with him. It sounds strange but it is true. It will also make him have what to discuss with you.

Getting to know about his career and passion does not mean having expertise knowledge of it, it means just enough to keep a conversation interesting. You can always know more by asking him; you will be surprised at the boring length he will go just to make you see how good he is in the field. Do not doze off, yawning is not even allowed.

To make him love you more, ask him what you can do to help him achieve his dreams faster. You will be registering yourself in his mind as a true "helpmeet".

- **Give him some space**

Do not be among the other girls who 'try to preserve their man'. This man is not yet yours and even if he has, he should be the one trying to preserve you. Clinging too tightly to a man before he tells you how he feels or even after it will end you in doom. You will lose the man and lose your respect before him.

I know you may be afraid of him meeting someone better who will take all his attention from you; you do not have to be. He knows what he sees in you before agreeing to talk to and create a bond with you.

Get out and be happy living your life and let him live his. When you meet again, you will have more to talk about. You will also be surprised how much of you he had missed. Know your value girl!

d) Master silence

We both know that silence is the loudest speaker, so why spend all your energy doing what you may never be able to do well? Remember an open mouth that pours out wisdom intrigued him, but what of a closed pair of lips that let him find the solution to the puzzle? Wouldn't that be damn exciting?

Do not tell him all your likes and dislikes, let him figure some out. Do not even tell him about your past relationships, if they were bad, they'll reduce your standard. Just keep your cool, be interesting, speak when it's necessary and lock up the lips when you are about to sell yourself off.

Silence will help you listen to him. Listen not to argue but to understand. Also, when you are both silent, your hearts will communicate and if your gazes are fixed, the heart will find its rhythm.

e) Develop patience

A lot of unforgettable women have missed opportunities of being with the man they so want because of the lack of this virtue. Lack of patience in life will not only cost you your man, but it can also cost you everything.

Love is a choice and men love to take their time before making that choice. If you happen to rush a guy to choose you, you will end up losing him. Here is how it works:

Have you ever had a guy that once asked you out but never allow you or your phone have peace because he wanted to get a yes from you? How did you feel? Troubled I guess. It is the same for a man. Rushing a man to make decisions of love will only make him disturbed, it will make him feel trapped and make you look desperate. That alone has robbed you of the chance of getting him. So in cases where the guy does not quickly get on to choosing you, what should you do? Wait.

What to do while waiting for prince charming to make up his mind

The only thing you can do while waiting for prince charming to decide whether or not he wants to be with you is to continue living your life. Do not forget that you are supposed to keep an open mind while trying to get his love.

Feel free to try new people; go out for dates. Since he has not yet made up his mind, you owe him no commitment. If hanging around others makes him jealous, he will hurry up and make you his and his alone.

You see, go with the flow and allow him to struggle blindly to find his way into your heart.

f) Let him be the man

By now, you should already be halfway into his head and if you want to reach that final destination, you have to let him do what men do or at least, believe he is doing so.

Let him pay for the dates, he's naturally a provider and this will show you how responsible he is. Let him protect you, though he may do that through jealousy. Let him lead, after all, you are already leading from the background.

For him to feel manly around you, you have to respect him. Do not talk back or raise your voice when he tries to make you mad. Chances are that he is just pushing your buttons. Walk away and keep your power and let him come back in his misery to apologize and seek for you.

Learn what makes him masculine and respect him. As the responsible man I believe he is, he will love to provide for and protect you. Let him. And in case he forgot his duties, pretend all is not well and get him back to his duty post.

g) Retreat

Babe, you've come a long way; congrats on your hard work but it's time to switch the baton. Let's really get him on the chasing role.

This retreat involves you ignoring a few calls from him and saying no to some of those mind-blowing dates. Yes, please give him the chance to miss you and wonder if you are going out with someone else. You are not to make him jealous, just let him wonder if there is a guy humping you when he's away. Don't feel guilty; you are not responsible for his thoughts. If he can't imagine you being with any other, he'll try to keep you for himself. Most often, he'll try to be unforgettable.

Isn't that cool? Now our most beloved Prince Charming is the one doing the work. He's helpless, believe me. Since he can't forget you, he's trying to make you feel the same for him. Hot!

h) Give in

Not completely though, but he'll be wary if he keeps seeking you without seeing anything tangible to hold on to. Let him have your care and a little of your love. Let there be a token to show him that his efforts will soon earn him the price.

Appreciate him and let him feel your warmth (of your soul, not necessarily your body). Make him feel safe with you. Let him know he's accepted and appreciated. Give him a reason to press on and not one to relax. If he loves the little he's getting from you, he'll lay down more to have all of you.

Give but don't 'shower' him with gifts. The gifts do not have to be mighty; they just have to carry your signature. You can make him some cookies or buy him a new key-holder; whatever the gift may be, let something in it convey information about you. If you chose a key-holder, it can be in the shape you love even if the color is a bit masculine. Don't forget, your gifts will speak your presence when you are absent.

CHAPTER 7 – Final Move

Love has always been a big decision and in as much we do want to have the love of our dream man so badly, we must not forget that he is also a person. Giving him the privilege to choose who he wants to love is very important.

This guide is enough to help you attract and keep any man of your choice. When you get him, do not forget to keep being the woman he chased. Or maybe I should put it this way: never forget to make him continue chasing you.

The mystery of getting a man is in being unforgettable; never let any man you meet forget you in just a split second.